REJECTED!

BY

DAVID MICHAEL PENA

DETICATION

TO CREATESPACE.COM FOR
PUBLISHING AND WEERACHON
KOSENANST FOR EDITING

INTRODUCTON

Now most of you know that have read any of my other books I tend to use foul language, because when I'm giving information I get real passionate about it and if that offends you

I'm Sorry and you might want to close this book now and phone you mommy. But if not then let's begin.

Now rejection is what we fear the most as sales people and can be the reason for us not hitting out goals. It is a proven fact that all human beings need to give and receive rejection to be psychologically healthy. You see most of us are sensitive individuals and are reluctant to express opinions, and tend to avoid arguments or controversial discussions, are reluctant to make requests or impose on others, because we are easily hurt by negative feedback from others, and we tend to rely too much on familiarity of others in most situations; so as to avoid rejection.

Why do we fear rejection so much? It's simple we don't like being told "no". People differ in their readiness to perceive and react to rejection. This causes an individual to have different reactions in rejection sensitivity and it not well understood why.

Although humans are social beings, it's a fact some levels of rejection is an inevitable part of life. So in our mind we think what if I knock on the door and the lady tells me fuck off out the yard? What if I make that sales call and the lady says "hey bitch you don't know I'm on the no call list"? What if the guy comes up to the lot to buy a car and I can't even sell him one. So what we do is justify knocking on that door at 8:45pm, oh its late and everyone is eating dinner, we'll just get a fresh start in the morning, or my favorite, it's almost time to go home so instead of making any sales calls I'll just shuffle papers around for the last hour. And we do all his in the fear of rejection.

Rejection no one likes, I don't and anyone who says they love rejection, and if they do, they probably need their head checked. The fact of the matter is in life is we are going to face rejection every day and even if not at work we will in our personal lives as well. Why are we scared to ask that girl or boy out on a date? Because we don't want to hear "well I'm washing my hair tonight". Once we here rejection it bothers us, and that's when doubt enters the equation and you cannot let this happen. We start think man no one's going to buy today and maybe my family was right I should just go get a "real job". The reason we are in sales is to become financial independent and own our own business and be able to give our family the things they deserve. If we start doubting our opportunity then we're finished. And this is what happens to us and that's why if you're in sales you have seen a number of people come and go in your office. Once doubt enters the equation you're on a path for destruction. So as sales people we need not do this. You have to understand your sales manager and boss have had some kind of success to get in the position they are in but sometimes we don't want to listen to them and do our own thing. If someone has the same product as you and is having more success than you, then there only one person to point the finger at and it's that person in the mirror. If you are reading this it means you are seeking out more information and trying to become better and you my friend are on the right path to success. I've been selling for 12 years and I'm going to teach you the things I know and have learned over the years but if you read most sales books the guy just tells you how great he is and how rich he is with never really giving you any information. Most of these guys never sold the just making money from a book by telling you how rich they are and everyone is rushing out to buy it. I'm a no BS kind of guy;

I'll tell you in a nut shell you can make money selling anything as long as you believe in the product and as long as you go out every day trying to sell it. Believing in your product is number one, don't think for a minute that a customer can't tell right away if you sincere about you product. Most direct sales companies will make you by the product then start selling it because if you have bought the product you believe in the product and you going to take the job more seriously,

The question is why does rejection bother

us so much, I was online to day pushing my books online and this guy got really nasty with me and that is what gave me the idea for this book. Let me tell you the story. I'm online networking with people as I do. Now the wake up now guys are always trying to friend me and get me to do then little operation and I'm really not sure what it is they even do, but I'm always nice and just kind of brush them off and today this guy (who is door to door salesman by the way), says I don't need no fucken book I have skill that's all I need and just being kind of snippy with me. Now when I used to knock on doors, I would run in these guys in the field. Now most of us will get mad and start a fight with these people. But if you want to really piss them off just be super nice and they won't know what to do you. You see this is what they want, a confrontation, but then I realized how much of an idiot he was when he said I solicit and I don't like to be solicited. Now that's a contradiction. You go out every day and knock on doors but now one is allowed to knock-on yours. Plus I know why he been a dealer for ever that's why he'll never make it to the next level because he's a knows-it-all. There is saying always stay green because you're growing once we become ripe we're rotten. Never stop learning because even though I like to think I have a lot of knowledge in the world of selling but I still read books and listen to tapes. It took a lot for me just to be nice and leave it alone but I'll tell you right now it's bothering him now because he realizes how much of an asshole he is. You see don't argue with stupid people, I've learned a long time ago you can't sell to a stupid person. The thing about common sense is it can't be taught you either have it of you don't.

Now the question comes well how do we not let rejection bother us and get butt hurt when someone tells us no. There is no secret, rejection will always bother us but I learned a long time of go in the world of selling it's not what happen to in life but it's how you deal with that matters. In the company I worked for we sang songs and did chants in the morning like most sales companies do. What this does is it gets us in the state of mind we need to handle rejection. Now if your company has some kind of song or chant, you must participate, don't be the guy that just mumbles through it like it's stupid. Companies do this for a reason, because it works. So get into and chant it like you mean it. This is my first rule of thumb, because you see what starts off right ends up right and what starts out wrong ends up wrong. Now if you knocking on doors or cold calling people you are going to get a lot of no's so you just have to face the fact you going to get rejected all day, if you one that goes into do presentations in someone's home, when you're finished you going to hear "no", if someone comes on the lot to look at cars, you might take them for a test drive even and then comeback, what are they going to tell you "NO". You'll find that the more pumped up you get in the morning the more rejection won't seem to bother you as much. Rejection has an impact on the emotional health and wellbeing of a person as well. Overall, experiments show that those who have been rejected will suffer from more negative emotions and have less positive emotions, so how do we break the cycle to have more positive emotions than negative emotions? Now reading positive materials when you have free time during the days will also help, now I have a book called 101 positive affirmations and I suggest you pick it up.

This is a book of inspirational quotes, some I made myself and some I have gotten from successful people. But what it does is keep you in the state of mind you need to be and be reminded of why you're doing the things you doing and who you are doing them for. Now the last thing you want to do is talk about all the negative shit that happen to you from the day before. Why do we do this? I think because it's fun. You see us being negative and telling a story about the lady that through a stick at you and told you to fuck off out of her yard, and we think we're being funny but, the subconscious mind doesn't know what to believe and where just spewing out negativity in our mind and to everyone else. If this is Joe Blows first day out of training and he here that story he out the back door and quitting before he ever gave himself a chance. So do not do this only speak of positive things from the day before. It kills me how we hate rejection so much and the next morning we focused on the negatives not the positives. Now I'm sure you've heard it before "be positive". But what does being positive really mean? It's plain and simple it means you when someone gets a sale, are we happy for them or do we say things like oh it was beginners luck or he probably sold it low and didn't make any money. Instead of telling them good job and asking them for some sales tips or about things they do in their presentations. Now I learned sometimes you can learn things from newer people, just because they have worked to company less time that you do not mean you can't learn something from them. If you a manger always be teaching and motivating your guys because they're going to go out to the field and have to face a lot of rejection. Now back to positivity, there is a thing I learned called PMA, it stands for positive mental attitude that is the most important thing in facing rejection. Now if we have been doing presentations all day and we haven't made a sale we have been rejected. Now these are the times positive mental attitude comes in, to keep us pushing for the late 8:30 presentation, now whatever we are selling knives, vacuums, solar panels, or alarms, a sale is not going to take place unless we are in a home. I was field manager and when I watched my guys and girls knock on doors, and I could tell right away who was going to get presentation and who was not. Just by the look on their face and by the way they moved. You see people pay attention to the way you look and your domineer. This is going to be the ultimate factor in the person letting you in to present your product. You ask how could I tell who was going to get a presentation and who wasn't? If the person would get out with that a sense of urgency, I mean walking fast and acting like they want to be there. The other one who wasn't going to get a presentation is the one that gets out slowly and shuts the door, "oh wait I forgot my pen", and then starts walking slowly down the street and looking around may be acting like he's writing something on his clip board. He just doesn't have the attitude right and like I said before you attitude is going to determine your outcome. Now everyone used to laugh at me because I used to run from door to door. Why did I do this? For two reasons I was out there to get into a house, because if I wasn't in a house presenting my product I had no way of making money and that's the way you have to look at it. So I recommend you try this work with some kind of urgency like you want to make something happen. Now don't think for a minute that people aren't looking at you from the gap in their curtains, and they want to waiting for you to come up to the door. Now I think this sparks some curiosity, now the people kind of want to open the door they want to see what this guy is so excited about that he's smiling and running from door to door. I'll tell you what by no way am I claiming to be the greatest but I can get into a house you can bet on that. So find something that keeps you attitude right for me it was working with a sense of urgency and I also sometimes would chant a positive quotes as I was knocking on doors, and there are a lot of them, if you would like some pick my other book 101 positive affirmations. One I like I'll share with you for free, I owe that much for buying this book I guess, I kid but here it goes

I want the best, I need the best, and I deserve the best that life has to offer. My family wants the best, my family needs the best, my family deserves the best that life has to offer

If get my other book there is a lot more where those come so you see the only way to fight rejection is get into a state of mind such great positivity that when we get rejected we just laugh about. Because if we let negative things affect our attitude that's when doubt enters the equation and we're finished. So find something positive to listen to or read. If you're reading these book congratulations you're on the path of success because you are seeking out information and that is what it takes a little investment in yourself and not on a 40oz. You see success is a journey not a destination.

Rejection will always affect us. If thought there was some magic thing I was going to tell you I'm sorry there is not one. The only way to handle rejections is participate in the chants in the morning. Whatever you do only speak of positive things. Don't be funny and talk about negative things that have happen to from the day before.

One thing that will help you is have a reason why. Why am I doing this? Why should I makes those last calls at 8:45 or knock that last street at 8:55 at night. What am I doing all this for? Now all of us have reason why. It could be to give our family the finer things in life and give them what they deserve. It could be because we want that nice sports car we always have dreamed of. It might be that we want to take our girlfriend or boyfriend on that contest trip to

Ensenada, Mexico. It could be just because we want to have enough in our savings account so that when problems arise we can take care of them, and not stress. You see I've learned money can't solve all you problems, but analyze all you problems right now and I'll bet you money can take care of 95% of them. Right? So find that reason why, write down you reason. There is a saying a man taught me a long time ago if you can think it ink it. You have to write your reason why down on paper put up in the office put it up in the bathroom mirror, put it up on the dashboard of your car so on the days when you attitude is not right you can remind yourself what you are doing it for.

Now one thing is a smile and I sure you've heard your boss and you managers say smile, but take it from some who's be selling door to door for 12 years, that they are absolutely right. A smile makes all the difference. Even if you on the phone don't think for a minute that the customer on the other end can't tell if you smiling or not. A smile is simple but so very important. Have you ever walked into a store and everyone is smiling and saying hello, and when you leave you say "I like this store I'm coming here more often". And when you walk into store and everyone just acts like they don't see as if they hope you don't ask them a question because they might actually have to get off the lazy ass and do something. Which store would you rather go to? Of course and we like the one where everyone is smiling. It always has amazed me I would be working in same area and the appointment setters would get an appointment and it was a house we have done before but didn't sell and sometimes we have even did the appointment 2 or 3 times, and My motto was I don't care how many presentations they have seen we'll keep doing until they buy. And the questions why would these people buy the 3rd time they have seen it, it's simple if the people don't like you, they will not buy from you. I never met someone that's said "we bought because the guy was a real asshole". Of Couse not we here the opposite, "he was such a nice guy". It's a proven fact the when you smile or laugh the other person will automatically imitate you. Try just go up to someone and start laughing hysterically and the will start to laugh too. You see smiling is contagious, and if the people are going to imitate us. What do we want a frowning prospect or a smiling prospect? Sure we would like a smiling one, and this goes for the same at the door, if you're smiling. The people think you're nice and they see you working hard so they take the free gift to let you do a presentation. Now I'm not saying everyone will let you in if you smile but I guarantee you average in the amount appointments you make will increase in VS the amount of doors you knock on, or the amount of calls you make.

Now rejection we are always going to fear because let's face it we would always rather here a yes than no. But in the world of selling most of the time we are going to hear more no's that yes's. So rejection is something we are guaranteed to have. The biggest thing is your attitude, that's what is going to keep us going on those days we don't have success and we have been doing presentations all day and everyone has rejected us. Are we going to keep a positive attitude and be there on time for the meeting tomorrow? Or are we going to pout and not come in the next day. So let's get out there make some sales, have some fun and I'll see you at the top!

Acknowledgement

If you have any thing you would like to add, feel free to like my facebook page and post a comment at

David Michael Pena

Author

www.facebook.com/autobiographyofdmp